A MATHEMATICIAN'S APOLOGY

G.H. HARDY

HAWK PRESS

Published by

Hawk Press

4836/24, Ansari Road, Daryaganj
New Delhi – 110 002
Phones : 9643330713, +91-11-23278618, +91-11-35676207
E-mail: thehawkpress@gmail.com
www.thehawkpress.com

ISBN: 978-93-88318-14-3

To

JOHN LOMAS

who asked me to write it

Preface

I am indebted for many valuable criticisms to Professor C. D. Broad and Dr C. P. Snow, each of whom read my original manuscript. I have incorporated the substance of nearly all of their suggestions in my text, and have so removed a good many crudities and obscurities.

In one case, I have dealt with them differently. My §28 is based on a short article which I contributed to *Eureka* (the journal of the Cambridge Archimedean Society) early in the year, and I found it impossible to remodel what I had written so recently and with so much care. Also, if I had tried to meet such important criticisms seriously, I should have had to expand this section so much as to destroy the whole balance of my essay. I have therefore left it unaltered, but have added a short statement of the chief points made by my critics in a note at the end.

G. H. H.

18 July, 1940

1

It is a melancholy experience for a professional mathematician to find himself writing about mathematics. The function of a mathematician is to do something, to prove new theorems, to add to mathematics, and not to talk about what he or other mathematicians havet done. Statesmen despise publicists, painters despise art-critics, and physiologists, physicists, or mathematicians have usually similar feelings: there is no scorn more profound, or on the whole more justifiable, than that of the men who make for the men who explain. Exposition, criticism, appreciation, is work for second-rate minds.

I can remember arguing this point once in one of the few serious conversations that I ever had with Housman. Housman, in his Leslie Stephen lecture *The Name and Nature of Poetry*, had denied very emphatically that he was a 'critic'; but he had denied it in what seemed to me a singularly perverse way, and had expressed an admiration for literary criticism which startled and scandalized me.

He had begun with a quotation from his inaugural lecture, delivered twenty-two years before—

> Whether the faculty of literary criticism is the best gift that Heaven has in its treasures, I cannot say; but Heaven seems to think so, for assuredly it is the gift most charily

> bestowed. Orators and poets…, if rare in comparison with blackberries, are commoner than returns of Halley's comet: literary critics are less common…

And he had continued—

> In these twenty-two years I have improved in some respects and deteriorated in others, but I have not so much improved as to become a literary critic, nor so much deteriorated as to fancy that I have become one.

It had seemed to me deplorable that a great scholar and a fine poet should write like this, and, finding myself next to him in Hall a few weeks later, I plunged in and said so. Did he really mean what he had said to be taken very seriously? Would the life of the best of critics really have seemed to him comparable with that of a scholar and a poet? We argued the questions all through dinner, and I think that finally he agreed with me. I must not seem to claim a dialectical triumph over a man who can no longer contradict me, but 'Perhaps not entirely' was, in the end, his reply to the first question, and 'Probably no' to the second.

There may have been some doubt about Housman's feelings, and I do not wish to claim him as on my side; but there is no doubt at all about the feelings of men of science, and I share them fully. If then I find myself writing, not mathematics, but 'about' mathematics, it is a confession of weakness, for which I may rightly be scorned or pitied by younger and more vigorous mathematicians. I write about mathematics because, like any other mathematician who has passed sixty, I have no longer the freshness of mind, the energy, or the patience to carry on effectively with my proper job.

2

I propose to put forward an apology for mathematics; and I may be told that it needs none, since there are now few studies more generally recognized, for good reasons or bad, as profitable and praiseworthy. This may be true: indeed it is probable, since the sensational triumphs of Einstein, that stellar astronomy and atomic physics are the only sciences which stand higher in popular estimation. A mathematician need not now consider himself on the defensive. He does not have to meet the sort of opposition described by Bradley in the admirable defence of metaphysics which forms the introduction to *Appearance and Reality*.

A metaphysician, says Bradley, will be told that 'metaphysical knowledge is wholly impossible', or that 'even if possible to acertain degree, it is practically no knowledge worth the name'. 'The same problems,' he will hear, 'the same disputes, the same sheer failure. Why not abandon it and come out? Is there nothing else worth your labour?' There is no one so stupid as to use this sort of language about mathematics.

The mass of mathematical truth is obvious and imposing; its practical applications, the bridges and steam-engines and dynamos, obtrude themselves on the dullest imagination. The public does not need to be convinced that there is something in mathematics.

All this is in its way very comforting to mathematicians, but it is hardly possible for a genuine mathematician to be content with it. Any genuine mathematician must feel that it is not on these crude achievements that the real case for mathematics rests, that the popular reputation of mathematics is based largely on ignorance and confusion, and there is room for a more rationaldefence. At any rate, I am disposed to try to make one. It should be a simpler task than Bradley's difficult apology.

I shall ask, then, why is it really worth while to make a serious study of mathematics? What is the proper justification of a mathematician's life? And my answers will be, for the most part, such as are expected from a mathematician: I think that it is worth while, that there is ample justification. But I should say at once that my defence of mathematics will be a defencc of myself, and that my apology is bound to be to some extent egotistical. I should not think it worth while to apologize for my subject if I regarded myself as one of its failures.

Some egotism of this sort is inevitable, and I do not feel that it really needs justification. Good work is not done by 'humble' men. It is one of the first duties of a professor, for example, in any subject, to exaggerate a little both the importance of his subject and his own importance in it. A man who is always asking 'Is what I do worth while?' and 'Am I the right person to do it?' will always be ineffective himself and a discouragement to others. He must shut his eyes a little and think a little more of his subject and himself than they deserve. This is not too difficult: it is harder not to make his subject and himself ridiculous by shutting his eyes too tightly.

3

A man who sets out to justify his existence and his activities has to distinguish two different questions. The first is whether the work which he does is worth doing; and the second is why he does it, whatever its value may be. The first question is often very difficult, and the answer very discouraging, but most people will find the second easy enough even then. Their answers, if they are honest, will usually take one or other of two forms; and the second form is a merely a humbler variation of the first, which is the only answer we need consider seriously.

(1) 'I do what I do because it is the one and only thing that I can do at all well. I am a lawyer, or a stockbroker, or a professional cricketer, because I have some real talent for that particular job. I am a lawyer because I have a fluent tongue, and am interested in legal subtleties; I am a stockbroker because my judgment of the markets is quick and sound; I am a professional cricketer because I can bat unusually well. I agree that it might be better to be a poet or a mathematician, but unfortunately I have no talent for such pursuits.

'I am not suggesting that this is a defence which can be made by most people, since most people can do nothing at all well. But it is impregnable when it can be made without absurdity, as it can by a substantial minority: perhaps five or even ten percent of men can do something rather well. It is a tiny minority who can do something *really* well, and the number of men who can do two things well is negligible. If a man has any genuine talent he should be ready to make almost any sacrifice in order to cultivate it to the full.

This view was endorsed by Dr Johnson

> When I told him that I had been to see [his namesake] Johnson ride upon three horses, he said 'Such a man, sir, should be encouraged, for his performances show the extent of the human powers ...'—

and similarly he would have applauded mountain climbers, channel swimmers, and blindfold chess-players. For my own part, I am entirely in sympathy with all such attempts at remarkable achievement. I feel some sympathy even with conjurors and ventriloquists and when Alekhine and Bradman set out to beat records, I am quite bitterly disappointed if they fail. And here both Dr. Johnson and I find ourselves in agreement with the public. As W. J. Turner has said so truly, it is only the 'highbrows' (in the unpleasant sense) who do not admire the 'real swells'.

We have of course to take account of the differences in value between different activities. I would rather be a novelist or a painter than a statesman of similar rank; and there are many roads to fame which most of us would reject as actively pernicious. Yet it is seldom that such differences of value will turn the scale in a man's choice of a career, which will almost always be dictated by the limitations of his natural abilities. Poetry is more valuable than cricket, but Bradman would be a fool if he sacrificed his cricket in order to write second-rate minor poetry (and I suppose that it is unlikely that he could do better). If the cricket were a little less supreme, and the poetry better, then the choice might be more difficult: I do not know whether I would rather have been Victor Trumper or Rupert Brooke. It is fortunate that such dilemmas are so seldom.

I may add that they are particularly unlikely to present themselves to a mathematician. It is usual to exaggerate rather grossly the differences between the mental processes of mathematicians and other people, but it is undeniable that a gift for mathematics is one of the most specialized talents, and that mathematicians as a class are not particularly distinguished for general ability or versatility. If a man is in any sense a real mathematician, then it is a hundred to one that his mathematics will be far better than anything else he can do, and that he would be silly if he surrendered any decent opportunity of exercising his one talent in order to do undistinguished work in other fields. Such a sacrifice could be justified only by economic necessity or age.

4

I had better say something here about this question of age, since it is particularly important for mathematicians. No mathematician should ever allow himself to forget that mathematics, more than any other art or science, is a young man's game. To take a simple illustration at a comparatively humble level, the average age of election to the Royal Society is lowest in mathematics. We can naturally find much more striking illustrations. We may consider, for example, the career of a man who was certainly one of the world's three greatest mathematicians. Newton gave up mathematics at fifty, and had lost his enthusiasm long before; he had recognized no doubt by the time he was forty that his greatest creative days were over. His greatest idea of all, fluxions and the law of gravitation, came to him about 1666, when he was twenty four—'in those days I was in the prime of my age for invention, and minded mathematics and philosophy more than at any time sine'. He made big discoveries until he was nearly forty (the 'elliptic orbit' at thirty-seven), but after that he did little but polish and perfect.

Galois died at twenty-one, Abel at twenty-seven, Ramanujan at thirty-three, Riemann at forty. There have been men who have done great work a good deal later; Gauss's great memoir on differential geometry was published when he was fifty (though he had had the fundamental ideas ten years before). I do not know an instance of a major mathematical advance initiated by a man past fifty. If a man of mature age loses interest in and abandons mathematics, the loss is not likely to be very serious either for mathematics or for himself.

On the other hand the gain is no more likely to be substantial: the later records of mathematicians are not particularly encouraging. Newton made a quite competent Master of the Mint (when he was not quarrelling with anybody). Painlevé was a not very successful Premier of France. Laplace's political career was highly discreditable, but he is hardly a fair instance since he was dishonest rather than incompetent, and never really 'gave up' mathematics. It is very hard to find an instance of a first-rate mathematician who has abandoned mathematics and attained first-rate distinction in any other field.[1] There may have been young men who would have been first-rate mathematician if they had stuck in mathematics, but I have never heard of a really plausible example. And all this is fully borne out by my very own limited experience. Every young mathematician of real talent whom I have known has been faithful to mathematics, and not from lack of ambition but from abundance of it; they have all recognized that there, if anywhere, lay the road to a life of any distinction.

[1] Pascal seems the best

5

There is also what I call the 'humbler variation' of the standard apology; but I may dismiss this in a very few words.

(2) 'There is *nothing* that I can do particularly well. I do what I do because it came my way. I really never had a chance of doing anything else.' And this apology too I accept as conclusive. It is quite true that most people can do nothing well. If so, it matters very little what career they choose, and there is really nothing more to say about it. It is a conclusive reply, but hardly one likely to be made by a man with any pride; and I may assume that none of us would be content with it.

6

It is time to begin thinking about the first question which I put in §3, and which is so much more difficult than the second. Is mathematics, what I and other mathematicians mean by mathematics, worth doing; and if so, why?

I have been looking again at the first pages of the inaugural lecture which I gave at Oxford in 1920, where there is an outline of an apology for mathematics. It is very inadequate (less than a couple of page), and is written in a style (a first essay, I suppose, in what I then imagined to be the 'Oxford manner') of which I am not now particularly proud; but I still feel that, however much development it may need, it contains the essentials of the matter. I will resume what I said then, as a preface to a fuller discussion.

(1) I began by laying stress on the *harmlessness* of mathematics—'the study of mathematics is, if an unprofitable, a perfectly harmless and innocent occupation'. I shall stick to that, but obviously it will need a good deal of expansion and explanation.

Is mathematics 'unprofitable'? In some ways, plainly, it is not; for example, it gives great pleasure to quite a large number of people. I was thinking of 'profit', however, in a narrower sense. Is mathematics 'useful', *directly* useful, as other sciences such as chemistry and physiology are? This is not an altogether easy or uncontroversial question, and I shall ultimately say No, though some mathematicians, and some outsiders, would no doubt say Yes. And is mathematics 'harmless'? Again the answer is not obvious, and the question is one which I should have in some ways preferred to avoid, since it raises the whole problem of the effect of science on war. Is mathematics harmless, in the sense in which, for example, chemistry plainly is not? I shall have to comeback to both these questions later.

(2) I went on to say that 'the scale of the universe is large and, if we are wasting our time, the waste of the lives of a few university dons is no such overwhelming catastrophe'; and here I may seem to be adopting, or affecting, the pose of exaggerated humility which I repudiated a moment ago. I am sure that that was not what was really in my mind: I was trying to say in a sentence that which I have said at much greater length in §3. I was assuming that we dons really had our little talents, and that we could hardly be wrong if we did our best to cultivate them further.

(3) Finally (in what seem to me now some rather painfully rhetorical sentences) I emphasized the permanence of mathematical achievement—

> What we do may be small, but it has a certain character of permanence; and to have produced anything of the slightest permanent interest, whether it be a copy of verses or a geometrical theorem, is to have done something utterly beyond the powers of the vast majority of men.

And—

In these days of conflict between ancient and modern studies, there must surely be something to be said for a study which did not begin with Pythagoras, and will not end with Einstein, but is the oldest and the youngest of all.

All this is 'rhetoric'; but the substance of it seems to me still to ring true, and I can expand on it at once without prejudicing any of the other questions which I am leaving open.

7

I shall assume that I am writing for readers who are full, or have in the past been full, of a proper spirit of ambition. A man's first duty, a young man's at any rate, is to be ambitious. Ambition is a noble passion which may legitimately take many forms; there was *something* noble in the ambitions of Attila or Napoleon; but the noblest ambition is that of leaving behind something of permanent value—

Here, on the level sand,
Between the sea and land,
What shall I build or write
Against the fall of night?

Tell me of runes to grave
That hold the bursting wave,
Or bastions to design,
For longer date than mine.

Ambition has been the driving force behind nearly all the best work of the world. In particular, practically all substantial contributions to human happiness have been made by ambitious men. To take two famous examples, were not Lister and Pasteur ambitions? Or, on a humbler level, King Gillette and William Willet; and who in recent times have contributed more to human comfort than they?

Physiology provides particularly good examples, just because it is so obviously a 'beneficial' study. We must guard against a fallacy common among apologist of science, the fallacy of supposing that the men whose work most benefits humanity are thinking much of that while they do it, that physiologists, for example, have particularly noble souls. A physiologist may indeed be glad to remember that his work will benefit mankind, but the motives which provide the force and the inspiration for it are indistinguishable from those of a classical scholar or a mathematician.

There are many highly respected motives which may lead men to prosecute research, but three which are much more important than the rest. The first (without which the rest must come to nothing) is intellectual curiosity, desire to know the truth. Then, professional pride, anxiety to be satisfied with one's performance, the shame that overcomes any self-respecting craftsman when his work is unworthy of his talent. Finally, ambition, desire for reputation, and the position, even the power or the money, which it brings. It may be fine to feel, when you have done your work, that you have added to the happiness or alleviated the sufferings of others, but that will not be why you did it. So if a mathematician, or a chemist, or even a physiologist, were to tell me that the driving force in his work had been the desire to benefit humanity, then I should not believe him (nor should I think the better of him if I did). His dominant motives have been those which I have stated, and in which, surely, there is nothing of which any decent man need be ashamed.

8

If intellectual curiosity, professional pride, and ambition are the dominant incentives to research, then assuredly no one has a fairer chance of satisfying them than a mathematician. His subject is the most curious of all—there is none in which truth plays such odd pranks. It has the most elaborate and the most fascinating technique, and gives unrivalled openings for the display of sheer professional skill. Finally, as history proves abundantly, mathematical achievement, whatever its intrinsic worth, is the most enduring of all.

We can see this even in semi-historic civilizations. The Babylonian and Assyrian civilizations have perished; Hammurabi, Sargon, and Nebuchadnezzar are empty names; yet Babylonian mathematics is still interesting, and the Babylonian scale of 60 is still used in astronomy. But of course the crucial case is that of the Greeks.

The Greeks were the first mathematicians who are still 'real' to us to-day. Oriental mathematics may be an interesting curiosity, but Greek mathematics is the real thing. The Greeks first spoke a language which modern mathematicians can understand: as Littlewood said to me once, they are not clever schoolboys or scholarship candidates', but 'Fellows of another college'. So Greek mathematics is 'permanent', more permanent even than Greek literature. Archimedes will be remembered when Aeschylus is forgotten, because languages die and mathematical ideas do not. 'Immortality' may be a silly word, but probably a mathematician has the best chance of whatever it may mean.

Nor need he fear very seriously that the future will be unjust to him. Immortality is often ridiculous or cruel: few of us would have chosen to be Og or Ananias or Gallio. Even in mathematics, history sometimes plays strange tricks; Rolle figures in the textbooks of elementary calculus as if he had been a mathematician like Newton; Farey is immortal because he failed to understand a theorem which Haros had proved perfectly fourteen years before; the names of five worthy Norwegians still stand in Abel's *Life*, just for one act of conscientious imbecility, dutifully performed at the expense of their country's greatest man. But on the whole the history of science is fair, and this is particularly true in mathematics. No other subject has such clear-cut or unanimously accepted standards, and the men who are remembered are almost always the men who merit it. Mathematical fame, if you have the cash to pay for it, is one of the soundest and steadiest of investments.

9

All this is very comforting for dons, and especially for professors of mathematics. It is sometimes suggested, by lawyers or politicians or business men, that an academic career is one sought mainly by cautious and unambitious persons who care primarily for comfort and security. The reproach is quite misplaced. A don surrenders something, and in particular the chance of making large sums of money—it is very hard for a professor to make £2000 a year; and security of tenure is naturally one of the considerations which make this particular surrender easy. That is not why Housman would have refused to be Lord Simon or Lord Beaverbrook. He would have rejected their careers because of his ambition, because he would have scorned to be a man forgotten in twenty years.

Yet how painful it is to feel that, with all these advantages, one may fail. I can remember Bertrand Russell telling me of a horrible dream. He was in the top floor of the University Library, about A.D. 2100. A library assistant was going round the shelves carrying an enormous bucket, taking down books, glancing at them, restoring them to the shelves or dumping them into the bucket. At last he came to three large volumes which Russell could recognize as the last surviving copy of *Principia Mathematica*. He took down one of the volumes, turned over a few pages, seemed puzzled for a moment by the curious symbolism, closed the volume, balanced it in his hand and hesitated....

10

A mathematician, like a painter or a poet, is a maker of patterns. If his patterns are more permanent than theirs, it is because they are made with *ideas*. A painter makes patterns with shapes and colours, a poet with words. A painting may embody an 'idea', but the idea is usually commonplace and unimportant. In poetry, ideas count for a good deal more; but, as Housman insisted, the importance of ideas in poetry is habitually exaggerated: 'I cannot satisfy myself that there are any such things as poetical ideas.... Poetry is not the thing said but a way of saying it.

> Not all the water in the rough rude sea
> Can wash the balm from an anointed King.

Could lines be better, and could ideas be at once more trite and more false? The poverty of the ideas seems hardly to affect the beauty of the verbal pattern. A mathematician, on the other hand, has no material to work with but ideas, and so his patterns are likely to last longer, since ideas wear less with time than words.

The mathematician's patterns, like the painter's or the poet's must be *beautiful*; the ideas like the colours or the words, must fit together in a harmonious way. Beauty is the first test: there is no permanent place in the world for ugly mathematics. And here I must deal with a misconception which is still widespread (though probably much less so now than it was twenty years ago), what Whitehead has called the 'literary superstition' that love of anaesthetic appreciation of mathematics is 'a monomania confined to a few eccentrics in each generation'.

It would be quite difficult now to find an educated man quite insensitive to the aesthetic appeal of mathematics. It may be very hard to *define* mathematical beauty, but that is just as true of beauty of any kind—we may not know quite what we mean by a beautiful poem, but that does not prevent us from recognizing one when we read it. Even Professor Hogben, who is out to minimize at all costs the importance of the aesthetic element in mathematics, does not venture to deny its reality. 'There are, to be sure, individuals for whom mathematics exercises a coldly impersonal attraction.... The aesthetic appeal of mathematics may be very real for a chosen few.' But they are 'few', he suggests, and they feel 'coldly' (and are really rather ridiculous people, who live in silly little university towns sheltered from the fresh breezes of the wide open spaces). In this he is merely echoing Whitehead's 'literary superstition'.

The fact is that there are few more 'popular' subjects than mathematics. Most people have some appreciation of mathematics, just as most people can enjoy a pleasant tune; and there are probably more people really interested in mathematics than in music. Appearances suggest the contrary, but there are easy explanations. Music can be used to stimulate mass emotion, while mathematics cannot; and musical incapacity is recognized (no doubt rightly) as mildly discreditable, whereas most people are so frightened of the name of mathematics that they are ready, quite unaffectedly, to exaggerate their own mathematical stupidity.

A very little reflection is enough to expose the absurdity of the 'literary superstition'. There are masses of chess-players in every civilized country—in Russia, almost the whole educatedpopulation; and every chess-player can recognize and appreciate a 'beautiful' game or problem. Yet a chess problem is *simply* an exercise in pure mathematics (a game not entirely, since psychology also plays a part), and everyone who calls a problem 'beautiful' is applauding mathematical beauty, even if it is a beauty of a comparatively lowly kind. Chess problems are the hymn-tunes of mathematics.

We may learn the same lesson, at a lower level but for a wider public, from bridge, or descending farther, from the puzzle columns of the popular newspapers. Nearly all their immense popularity is a tribute to the drawing power of rudimentary mathematics, and the better makers of puzzles, such as Dudeney or 'Caliban', use very little else. They know their business: whatthe public wants is a little intellectual 'kick', and nothing else has quite the kick of mathematics.

I might add that there is nothing in the world which pleases even famous men (and men who have used quite disparaging words about mathematics) quite so much as to discover, or rediscover, a genuine mathematical theorem. Herbert Spencer republished in his autobiography a theorem about circles which he proved when he was twenty (not knowing that it had been proved over two thousand years before by Plato). Professor Soddy is a more recent and more striking example (but his theorem really is his own).[2]

---

[2] See his letter on the 'Hexlet' in *Nature*, vols. 127-9 (1936-7)

11

A chess problem is genuine mathematics, but it is in some way 'trivial' mathematics. However ingenious and intricate, however original and surprising the moves, there is something essential lacking. Chess problems are *unimportant*. The best mathematics is *serious* as well as beautiful—'important' if you like, but the word is very ambiguous, and 'serious' expresses what I meanmuch better.

I am not thinking of the 'practical' consequences of mathematics. I have to return to that later: at present I will say only that if a chess problem is, in the crude sense, 'useless', then that is equally true of most of the best mathematics; that very little of mathematics is useful practically, and that that little is comparatively dull. The 'seriousness' of a mathematical theorem lies, not in its practical consequences, which are usually negligible, but in the *significance* of the mathematical ideas which it connects. We may say, roughly, that a mathematical idea is 'significant' if it can be connected, in a natural and illuminating way, with a large complex of other mathematical ideas. Thus a serious mathematical theorem, a theorem which connects significant ideas, is likely to lead to important advance in mathematics itself and even in other sciences. No chess problem has ever affected the general development of scientific thought: Pythagoras, Newton, Einstein have in their times changed its whole direction.

The seriousness of a theorem, of course, does not *lie* in its consequences, which are merely the *evidence* for its seriousness. Shakespeare had an enormous influence on the development of the English language, Otway next to none, but that is not why Shakespeare was the better poet. He was the better poet because he wrote much better poetry. The inferiority of the chess problem, like that of Otway's poetry, lies not in its consequences but in its content.

There is one more point which I shall dismiss very shortly, not because it is uninteresting but because it is difficult, and because I have no qualifications for any serious discussion in aesthetics. The beauty of a mathematical theorem *depends* a great deal on its seriousness, as even in poetry the beauty of a line may depend to some extent on the significance of the ideas which it contains. I quoted two lines of Shakespeare as an example of the sheer beauty of a verbal pattern, but.

After life's fitful fever he sleeps well

seems still more beautiful. The pattern is just as fine, and in this case the ideas have significance and the thesis is sound, so that our emotions are stirred much more deeply. The ideas do matterto the pattern, even in poetry, and much more, naturally, in mathematics; but I must not try to argue the question seriously.

12

It will be clear by now that, if we are to have any chance of making progress, I must produce example of 'real' mathematical theorems, theorems which every mathematician will admit to be first-rate. And here I am very handicapped by the restrictions under which I am writing. On the one hand my examples must be very simple, and intelligible to a reader who has no specialized mathematical knowledge; no elaborate preliminary explanations must be needed; and a reader must be able to follow the proofs as well as the enunciations. These conditions exclude, for instance, many of the most beautiful theorems of the theory of numbers, such as Fermat's 'two square' theorem on the law of quadratic reciprocity. And on the other hand my examples should be drawn from the 'pukka' mathematics, the mathematics of the working professional mathematician; and this condition excludes a good deal which it would be comparatively easy to make intelligible but which trespasses on logic and mathematical philosophy.

I can hardly do better than go back to the Greeks. I will state and prove two of the famous theorems of Greek mathematics. They are 'simple' theorems, simple both in idea and in execution, but there is no doubt at all about their being theorems of the highest class. Each is as fresh and significant as when it has discovered—two thousand years have not written a wrinkle on either of them. Finally, both the statements and the proofs can be mastered in an hour by any intelligent reader, however slender his mathematical equipment.

1. The first is Euclid's[3] proof of the existence of an infinity of prime numbers.

The *prime numbers* or *primes* are the numbers

(A) 2, 3, 5, 7, 11, 13, 17, 19, 23, 29,...

which cannot be resolved into smaller factors[4]. Thus 37 and 317 are prime. The primes are the material out of which all numbers are built up by multiplication: thus 666 = 2 · 3 · 3 · 37. Every number which is not prime itself is divisible by at least one prime (usually, of course, by several). We have to prove that there are infinitely many primes, i.e. that the series (A) never comes to an end.

Let us suppose that it does, and that

$$2, 3, 5, \ldots, P$$

is the complete series (so that P is the largest prime); and let us, on this hypothesis, consider the number Q defined by the formula

$$Q = (2.\ 3.\ 5 \ldots P) + 1.$$

It is plain that Q is not divisible by and of 2, 3, 5,..., P; for it leaves the remainder 1 when divided by any one of these numbers. But, if not itself prime, it is divisible by *some* prime, and therefore there is a prime (which may be Q itself) greater

[3] *Elements* IX 20. The real origin of many theorems in the *Elements* is obscure, and there seems to be no particular reason for supposing that this one is not Euclid's own.

[4] There are technical reasons for not counting 1 as a prime.

than any of them. This contradicts our hypothesis, that there is no prime greater than P; and therefore this hypothesis is false.

The proof is by *reductio ad absurdum*, and *reductio ad absurdum*, which Euclid loved so much, is one of a mathematician's finest weapons[5]. It is a far finer gambit than any chess gambit: a chess player may offer the sacrifice of a pawn or even a piece, but a mathematician offers *the game*.

[5] The proof can be arranged so as to avoid a *reductio*, and logicians of some schools would prefer that it should be.

13

2. My second example is Pythagoras's's[6] proof of the 'irrationality' of $\sqrt{2}$. A 'rational number' is fraction $\frac{a}{b}$, where *a* and *b* are integers: we may suppose that *a* and *b* have no common factor, since if they had we could remove it. To say that $\sqrt{2}$ is irrational' is merely another way of saying that 2 cannot be expressed in the form $\left(\frac{a}{b}\right)^2$; and this is the same as saying that the equation

$$a^2 = 2b^2 \qquad \text{(B)}$$

cannot be satisfied by integral values of *a* and *b* which have no common factor. This is a theorem of pure arithmetic, which does not demand any knowledge of 'irrational numbers' or depend on any theory about their nature.

We argue again by *reductio ad absurdum*; we suppose that (B) is true, *a* and *b* being integers without any common factor. It follows from (B) that a^2 is even (since $2b^2$ is divisible by 2), and therefore that *a* is even (since the square of an odd number is odd). If *a* is even then

$$a = 2c \qquad \text{(C)}$$

[6] The proof traditionally ascribed to Pythagoras, and certainly a product of his school. The theorem occurs, in a much more general form, in Euclid (Elements X 9).

for some integral value of c; and therefore

$$2b^2 = a^2 = (2c)^2 = 4c^2$$

or

(D) $$b^2 = 2c^2$$

Hence b^2 is even, and therefore (for the same reason as before) b is even. That is to say, a and b are both even, and so have common factor 2. This contradicts our hypothesis, and therefore the hypothesis is false.

It follows from Pythagoras's theorem that the diagonal of a square is in commensurable with the side (that their ratio is not a rational number, that there is no unit of which both are integral multiples). For if we take the side as our unit of length, and the length of the diagonal is d, then, by a very familiar theorem also ascribed to Pythagoras[7],

$$d^2 = 1^2 + 1^2 = 2$$

So that d cannot be a rational number.

I could quote any number of fine theorems from the theory of numbers whose *meaning* anyone can understand. For example, there is what is called 'the fundamental theorem of arithmetic', that any integer can be resolved, *in one way only*, into a product of primes. Thus 666 = 2· 3· 3· 37, and there is no other decomposition; it is impossible that 666 = 2 · 11· 29 or that 13· 89 = 17· 73 (and we can see so without working out the products). This theorem is, as its name implies, the foundation of higher arithmetic; but the proof, although not 'difficult',

[7], Euclid, Elements I 47.

requires a certain amount of preface and might be found tedious by an unmathematical reader.

Another famous and beautiful theorem is Fermat's 'two square' theorem. The primes may (if we ignore the special prime 2) be arranged in two classes; the primes

$$5, 13, 17, 29, 37, 41, \ldots$$

which leave remainder 1 when divided by 4, and the primes

$$3, 7, 11, 19, 23, 31, \ldots$$

which leave remainder 3. All the primes of the first class, and none of the second, can be expressed as the sum of two integral squares: thus

$$5 = 1^2 + 2^2, \qquad 13 = 2^2 + 3^2,$$

$$17 = 1^2 + 4^2, \qquad 29 = 2^2 + 5^2;$$

but 3, 7, 11, and 19 are not expressible in this way (as the reader may check by trial). This is Fermat's theorem, which is ranked, very justly, as one of the finest of arithmetic. Unfortunately, there is no proof within the comprehension of anybody but a fairly expert mathematician.

There are also beautiful theorems in the 'theory of aggregates' (*Mengenlehre*), such as Cantor's theorem of the 'non enumerability' of the continuum. Here there is just the opposite difficulty. The proof is easy enough, when once the language has been mastered, but considerable explanation is necessary before the meaning of the theorem becomes clear. So I will not try to give more examples. Those which I have given are test cases, and a reader who cannot appreciate them is unlikely to appreciate anything in mathematics.

I said that a mathematician was a maker of patterns of ideas, and that beauty and seriousness were the criteria by which his patterns should be judged. I can hardly believe that anyone who has understood the two theorems will dispute that they pass these tests. If we compare them with Dudeney's most ingenious puzzles, or the finest chess problems the masters of that art have composed, their superiority in both respects stands out: there is an unmistakable difference of class. They are much more serious, and also much more beautiful: can define, a little more closely, where their superiority lies?

14

In the first place, the superiority of the mathematical theorems in *seriousness* is obvious and over-whelming. The chess problem is the product of an ingenious but very limited complex of ideas, which do not differ from one another very fundamentally and have no external repercussions. We should think in the same way if chess had never been invented, whereas the theorems of Euclid and Pythagoras have influenced thought profoundly, even outside mathematics.

Thus Euclid's theorem is vital for the whole structure of arithmetic. The primes are the raw material out of which we have to build arithmetic, and Euclid's theorem assures us that we haveplenty of material for the task. But the theorem of Pythagoras has wider applications and provides a better text.

We should observe first that Pythagoras's argument is capable of far reaching extension, and can be applied, with little change of principle to very wide classes of 'irrationals'. We can prove very similarly (as Theaetetus seems to have done) that

$$\sqrt{3}, \sqrt{5}, \sqrt{11}, \sqrt{13}, \sqrt{17}$$

are irrational, or (going beyond Theaetetus) that $\sqrt[3]{2}$ and $\sqrt[3]{17}$ are irrational[8].

Euclid's theorem tells us that we have a good supply of material for the construction of a coherent arithmetic of the integers. Pythagoras's theorem and its extensions tell us that, when wehave constructed this arithmetic, it will not prove sufficient for our needs, since there will be many magnitudes which obtrude themselves upon our attention and which it will be unable to measure: the diagonal of the square is merely the most obvious example. The profound importance of this discovery was recognized at once by the Greek mathematicians. They had begun by assuming (in accordance, I suppose, with the 'natural' dictates of 'common sense') that all magnitudes of the same kind are commensurable, that any two lengths, for example, are multiples of some common unit, and they had constructed a theory of proportion based on this assumption. Pythagoras's discovery exposed the unsoundness of this foundation, and led to the construction of the much more profound theory of Eudoxus which is set out in the fifth book of the *Elements*, and which is regarded by many modern mathematicians as the finest achievement of Greek mathematics. The theory is astonishingly modern in spirit, and may be regarded as the beginning of the modern theory of irrational number, which has revolutionizzed mathematical analysis and had much influence on recent philosophy.

There is no doubt at all, then, of the 'seriousness' of either theorem. It is therefore the better worth remarking that neither theorem has the slightest 'practical' importance. In practical

---

[8] See Ch. IV of Hardy and Wright's *Introduction to the Theory of Numbers*, where there are discussions of different generalizations of Pythagoras's argument, and of a historical puzzled about Theaetetus.

application we are concerned only with comparatively small numbers; only stellar astronomy and atomic physics deal with 'large' numbers, and they have very little more practical importance, as yet, than the most abstract pure mathematics. I donot know what is the highest degree of accuracy ever useful to an engineer—we shall be very generous if we say ten significant figures. Then

$$3.14159265$$

(the value of π to eight places of decimals) is the ratio

$$\frac{314159265}{1000000000}$$

of two numbers of ten digits. The number of primes less than 1,000,000,000 is 50,847,478 : that is enough for an engineer, and he can be perfectly happy without the rest. So much for Euclid's theorem; and, as regards Pythagoras's, it is obvious that irrationals are uninteresting to an engineer, since he is concerned only with approximations, and all approximations are rational.

15

A 'serious' theorem is a theorem which contains 'significant' ideas, and I suppose that I ought to try to analyse a little more closely the qualities which make a mathematical idea significant. This is very difficult, and it is unlikely that any analysis which I can give will be very valuable. We can recognize a 'significant' idea when we see it, as we can those which occur in my two standard theorems; but this power of recognition requires a high degree of mathematical sophistication, and of that familiarity with mathematical ideas which comes only from many years spent in their company. So I must attempt some sort of analysis; and it should be possible to make one which, however inadequate, is sound and intelligible so far as it goes. There are two things at any rate which seem essential, a certain *generality* and a certain *depth*; but neither quality is easy to define at all precisely.

A significant mathematical idea, a serious mathematical theorem, should be 'general' in some such sense as this. The idea should be one which is a constituent in many mathematical constructs, which is used in the proof of theorems of many different kinds. The theorem should be one which, even if stated originally (like Pythagoras's theorem) in a quite special form, is capable of considerable extension and is typical of a whole class of theorems of its kind. The relations revealed by the proof should be such as to connect many different mathematical ideas. All this is very vague, and subject to many reservations. But it is easy enough to see that a theorem is unlikely to be serious when it lacks these qualities conspicuously; we have only to take examples from the isolated curiosities in which arithmetic abounds. I take two, almost at random, from Rouse Ball's *Mathematical Recreations*[9].

(a) 8712 and 9801 are the only four-figure numbers which are integral multiples of their 'reversals':

$$8712 = 4 \cdot 2178, \quad 9801 = 9 \cdot 1089$$

and there are no other numbers below 10,000 which have this property.

(b) There are just four number (after 1) which are the sums of the cubes of their digits, viz.

$$153 = 1^3 + 5^3 + 3^3, \qquad 370 = 3^3 + 7^3 + 0^3,$$

$$371 = 3^3 + 7^3 + 1^3, \qquad 407 = 4^3 + 0^3 + 7^3.$$

These are odd facts, very suitable for puzzle columns and likely to amuse amateurs, but there is nothing in them which appeals much to a mathematician. The proofs are neither difficult nor interesting—merely a little tiresome. The theorems are not serious; and it is plain that one reason (though perhaps not the most important) is the extreme speciality of both the enunciations and the proofs, which are not capable of any significant generalization.

[9] 11th edition, 1939 (revised by H. S. M. Coxeter).

16

'Generality' is an ambiguous and rather dangerous word, and we must be careful not to allow it to dominate our discussion too much. It is used in various senses both in mathematics and in writings about mathematics, and there is one of these in particular, on which logicians have very properly laid great stress, which is entirely irrelevant here. In this sense, which is quite easy to define, *all* mathematical theorems are equally and completely general.

'The certainty of mathematics', says Whitehead[10], 'depends on its complete abstract generality.' When we assert that 2 + 3 = 5, we are asserting a relation between three groups of 'things'; and these 'things' are not apples or pennies, or things of any one particular sort or another, but *just* things, 'any old things'. The meaning of the statement is entirely independent of the individualities of the members of the groups. All mathematical 'objects' or 'entities' or 'relations', such as '2', '3', '4', ' + ', or ' = ', and all mathematical propositions in which they occur, are completely general in the sense of being completely abstract. Indeed one of Whitehead's words is superfluous, since generality, in this sense, *is* abstractness.

This sense of the word is important, and the logicians are quite right to stress it, since it embodies a truism which a good

[10] *Science and the Modern World*, p. 33.

many people who ought to know better are apt to forget. It is quite common, for example, for an astronomer or a physicist to claim that he has found a 'mathematical proof' that the physical universe must behave in a particular way. All such claim, if interpreted literally, are strictly nonsense. It *cannot* be possible to prove mathematically that there will be an eclipse tomorrow, because eclipses, and other physical phenomena, do not form part of the abstract world of mathematics; and this, I suppose, all astronomers would admit when pressed, however many eclipses they may have predicted correctly.

It is obvious that we are not concerned with this sort of 'generality'now. We are looking for *differences* of generality between one mathematical theorem and another, and in Whitehead's sense all are equally general. Thus the 'trivial' theorems (a) and (b) of §15 are just as 'abstract' or 'general' as those of Euclid and Pythagoras, and so is a chess problem. It makes no difference to achess problem whether the pieces are white and black, or red and green, or whether there are physical 'pieces' at all; it is the *same* problem which an expert carries easily in his head and which we have to reconstruct laboriously with the aid of the board. The board and the pieces are mere devices to stimulate our sluggish imaginations, and are no more essential to the problem than the blackboard and the chalk are to the theorems in a mathematical lecture.

It is not this kind of generality, common to all mathematical theorems, which we are looking for now, but the more subtle and elusive kind of generality which I tried to describe in rough terms in §15. And we must be careful not to lay *too* much stress even on generality of this kind (as I think logicians like

Whitehead tend to do). It is not mere 'piling of subtlety of generalization upon subtlety of generalization'[11] which is the outstanding achievement of modern mathematics. Some measure of generality must be present in any high-class theorem, but *too much* tends inevitably to insipidity. 'Everything is what it is, and not another thing', and the differences between things are quite as interesting as their resemblances. We do not choose our friends because they embody all the pleasant qualities of humanity, but because they are the people that they are. And so in mathematics; a propertycommon to too many objects can hardly be very exciting, and mathematical ideas also become dim unless they have plenty of individuality. Here at any rate I can quote Whitehead on my side: 'it is the large generalization, limited by a happy particularity,which is the fruitful conception.[12]

---

[11] Science and the Modern World, p. 44.

[12] Science and the Modern World, p. 46.

17

The second quality which I demanded in a significant idea was *depth*, and this is still more difficult to define. It has *something* to do with *difficulty*; the 'deeper' ideas are usually the harder to grasp: but it is not at all the same. The ideas underlying Pythagoras's theorem and its generalization are quite deep, but no mathematicians now would find them difficult. On the other hand a theorem may be essentially superficial and yet quite difficult to prove (as are many 'Diophantine' theorems, i.e. theorems about the solution of equations in integers).

It seems that mathematical ideas are arranged somehow in strata, the ideas in each stratum being linked by a complex of relations both among themselves and with those above and below. The lower the stratum, the deeper (and in general more difficult) the idea. Thus the idea of an 'irrational' is deeper than that of an integer; and Pythagoras's theorem is, for that reason, deeper than Euclid's.

Let us concentrate our attention on the relations between the integers, or some other group of objects lying in some particular stratum. Then it may happen that one of these relations can be comprehended completely, that we can recognize and prove, for example, some property of the integers, without any knowledge of the contents of lower strata. Thus we proved Euclid's theorem by consideration of properties of integers only. But there are also many theorems about integers which we cannot appreciate properly, and still less prove, without digging deeper and considering what happens below.

It is easy to find examples in the theory of prime numbers. Euclid's theorem is very important, but not very deep: we can prove that there are infinitely many primes without using any notion deeper than that of 'divisibility'. But new questions suggest themselves as soon as we know the answer to this one. There is an infinity of primes, but how is the infinity distributed? Given a large number N, say 10^{80} or $10^{10^{10}}$,[13] about how many primes are there less than N?[14] When we ask *these* questions, we find ourselves in a different position. We can answer them, with rather surprising accuracy, but only by boring much deeper, leaving the integers above us for a while, and using the most powerful weapons of the modern theory of functions. Thus the theorem which answers our questions (the so-called 'Prime Number Theorem') is a much deeper theorem than Euclid's or even Pythagoras's.

I could multiply examples, but this notion of 'depth' is an elusive one even for a mathematician who can recognize it, and I can hardly suppose that I could say anything more about it here that would be of much help to other readers.

---

[13] It is supposed that the number of protons in the universe is about 10^{80}. The number $10^{10^{10}}$, if written at length, would occupy about 50,000 volumes of average size.

[14] As I mentioned in §14, there are 50,847,478 primes less than 1,000,000,000; but that is as far as our *exact* knowledge extends.

18

There is still one point remaining over from §11, where I started the comparison between 'real mathematics' and chess. We may take it for granted now that in substance, seriousness, significance, the advantage of the real mathematical theorem is overwhelming. It is almost equally obvious, to a trained intelligence, that it has a great advantage in beauty also; but this advantage is much harder to define or locate, since the *main* defect of the chess problem is plainly its 'triviality', and the contrast in this respect mingles with and disturbs any more purely aesthetic judgement. What 'purely aesthetic' qualities can we distinguish in such theorems as Euclid's or Pythagoras's? I will not risk more than a few disjointed remarks.

In both theorems (and in the theorems, of course, I include the proofs) there is a very high degree of *unexpectedness*, combined with *inevitability* and *economy*. The arguments take so odd and surprising a form; the weapons used seem so childishly simple when compared with the far-reaching results; but there is no escape from the conclusions. There are no complications of detail—one line of attack is enough in each case; and this is true too of the proofs of many much more difficult theorems, the full appreciation of which demands quite a high degree of technical proficiency. We do not want many 'variations' in the proof of a mathematical theorem: 'enumeration of cases', indeed, is one of the duller forms of mathematical argument. A mathematical proof should resemble a simple and clear-cut constellation, not a scattered cluster in the Milky Way.

A chess problem also has unexpectedness, and a certain economy; it is essential that the moves should be surprising, and that every piece of the board should play its part. But the aesthetic effect is cumulative. It is essential also (unless the problem is too simple to be really amusing) that the key-move should be followed by a good many variations, each requiring its own individual answer. 'If P-B5 then Kt-R6; if .... then ....; if .... then....'— the effect would be spoilt if there were not a good many different replies. All this is quite genuine mathematics, and has its merits; but it is just that 'proof by enumeration of cases' (and of cases which do not, at bottom, differ at all profoundly[15]) which areal mathematician tends to despise.

I am inclined to think that I could reinforce my argument by appealing to the feelings of chess-players themselves. Surely a chess master, a player of great games and great matches, at bottom scorns a problemist's purely mathematical art. He has much of it in reserve himself, and can produce it in an emergency: 'if he had made such and such a move, then I had such and such a winning combination in mind.' But the 'great game' of chess is primarily psychological, a conflict between one trained intelligence and another, and not a mere collection of small mathematical theorems.

---

[15] I believe that it is now regarded as a merit in a problem that there should be many variations of the same type.

19

I must return to my Oxford apology, and examine a little more carefully some of the points which I postponed in §6. It will be obvious by now that I am interested in mathematics only as a creative art. But there are other questions to be considered, and in particular that of the 'utility' (or uselessness) of mathematics, about which there is much confusion of thought. We must also consider whether mathematics is really quite so 'harmless' as I took for granted in my Oxford lecture.

A science or an art may be said to be 'useful' if its development increases, even indirectly, the material well-being and comfort of men, if it promotes happiness, using that word in a crude and common place way. Thus medicine and physiology are useful because they relieve suffering, and engineering is useful because it helps us to build houses and bridges, and so to raise the standard of life (engineering, of course, does harm as well, but that is not the question at the moment). Now some mathematics is certainly useful in this way; the engineers could not do their job without a fair working knowledge of mathematics, and mathematics is beginning to find applications even in physiology. So here we have a possible ground for a defence of mathematics; it may not be the best, or even a particularly strong defence, but it is one which we must examine. The 'nobler' uses of mathematics, if such they be, the uses which it shares with all creative art, will be irrelevant to our examination. Mathematics may, like poetry or music, 'promote and sustain a lofty habit of mind', and so increase the happiness of mathematicians and even of other people; but to defend it on that ground would be merely to elaborate what I have said already. What we have to consider now is the 'crude' utility of mathematics.

20

All this may seem very obvious, but even here there is often a good deal of confusion, since the most 'useful' subjects are quite commonly just those which it is most useless for most of us to learn. It is useful to have an adequate supply of physiologists and engineers; but physiology and engineering are not useful studies for ordinary men (though their study may of course be defended on other grounds). For my own part I have never once found myself in a position where such scientific knowledge as I possess, outside pure mathematics, has brought me the slightest advantage.

It is indeed rather astonishing how little practical value scientific knowledge has for ordinary men, how dull and common place such of it as has value is, and how its value seems almost to vary inversely to its reputed utility. It is useful to be tolerably quick at common arithmetic (and that, of course, is pure mathematics). It is useful to know a little French or German, a little history and geography, perhaps even a little economics. But a little chemistry, physics, or physiology has no value at all in ordinary life. We know that the gas will burn without knowing its constitution; when our cars break down we take them to a garage; when our stomach is out of order, we go to a doctor or a drug store. We live either by rule of thumb or on other people's professional knowledge.

However, this is a side issue, a matter of pedagogy, interesting only to school masters who have to advise parents clamouring for a 'useful' education for their sons. Of course we do not mean, when we say that physiology is useful, that most people ought to study physiology, but that the development of physiology by a handful of experts will increase the comfort of the majority. The questions which are important for us now are, how far mathematic scan claim this sort of utility, what kinds of mathematics can make the strongest claims, and how far the intensive study of mathematics, as it is understood by mathematicians, can be justified on this ground alone.

21

It will probably be plain by now to what conclusions I am coming; so I will state them at once dogmatically and then elaborate them a little. It is undeniable that a good deal of elementary mathematics—and I use the word 'elementary' in the sense in which professional mathematicians use it, in which it includes, for example, a fair working knowledge of the differential and integral calculus—has considerable practical utility. These parts of mathematics are, on the whole, rather dull; they are just the parts which have the least aesthetic value. The 'real' mathematics of the 'real' mathematicians, the mathematics of Fermat and Euler and Gauss and Abel and Riemann, is almost wholly 'useless' (and this is as true of 'applied' as of 'pure' mathematics). It is not possible to justify the life of any genuine professional mathematician on the ground of the 'utility' of his work.

But here I must deal with a misconception. It is sometimes suggested that pure mathematicians glory in the uselessness of their work[16], and make it a boast that it has no practical

[16] I have been accused of taking this view myself. I once said that 'a science is said to be useful if its development tends to accentuate the existing inequalities in the distribution of wealth, or more directly promotes the destruction of human life', and this sentence, written in 1915, has been quoted (for or against me) several times. It was of course a conscious rhetorical flourish, though one perhaps excusable at the time when it was written.

applications. The imputation is usually based on an incautious saying attributed to Gauss, to the effect that, if mathematics is the queen of the sciences, then the theory of numbers is, because of its supreme uselessness, the queen of mathematics—I have never been able to find an exact quotation. I am sure that Gauss's saying (if indeed it be his) has been rather crudely misinterpreted. If the theory of numbers could be employed for any practical and obviously honourable purpose, if it could be turned directly to the furtherance of human happiness or the relief of human suffering, as physiology and even chemistry can, then surely neither Gauss nor any other mathematician would have been so foolish as to decry or regret such applications. But science works for evil as well as for good (and particularly, of course, in time of war); and both Gauss and less mathematicians may be justified in rejoicing that there is one science at any rate, and that their own, whose very remoteness from ordinary human activities should keep it gentle and clean.

22

There is another misconception against which we must guard. It is quite natural to suppose that there is a great difference in utility between 'pure' and 'applied' mathematics. This is a delusion: there is a sharp disctinction between the two kinds of mathematics, which I will explain in a moment, but it hardly affects their utility.

How do pure and applied mathematicians differ from one another? This is a question which can be answered definitely and about which there is general agreement among mathematicians. There will be nothing in the least unorthodox about my answer, but it needs a little preface.

My next two sections will have a mildly philosophical flavour. The philosophy will not cut deep, or be in any way vital to my main theses; but I shall use words which are used very frequently with definite philosophical implications, and a reader might well become confused if I did not explain how I shall use them.

I have often used the adjective 'real', and as we use it commonly in conversation. I have spoken of 'real mathematics' and 'real mathematicians', as I might have spoken of 'real poetry' or 'real poets', and I shall continue to do so. But I shall also use the word 'reality', and with two different connotations.

In the first place, I shall speak of 'physical reality', and here again I shall be using the word in the ordinary sense. By physical reality I mean the material world, the world of day and night, earthquakes and eclipses, the world which physical science tries to describe.

I hardly suppose that, up to this point, any reader is likely to find trouble with my language, but now I am near to more difficult ground. For me, and I suppose for most mathematicians, there is another reality, which I will call 'mathematical reality'; and there is no sort of agreement about the nature of mathematical reality among either mathematicians or philosophers. Some hold that it is 'mental' and that in some sense we construct it, others that it is outside and independent of us. A man who could give a convincing account of mathematical reality would have solved very many of the most difficult problems of metaphysics. If he could include physical reality in his account, he would have solved them all.

I should not wish to argue any of these questions here even if I were competent to do so, but I will state my own position dogmatically in order to avoid minor misapprehensions. I believe that mathematical reality lies outside us, that our function is to discover or *observe* it, and that the theorems which we prove, and which we describe grandiloquently as our 'creations', are simply our notes of our observations. This view has been held, in one form or another, by many philosophers of high reputation from Plato onwards, and I shall use the language which is natural to a man who holds it. A reader who does not the philosophy can alter the language: it will make very little difference to my conclusions.

23

The contrast between pure and applied mathematics stands out most clearly, perhaps, in geometry. There is the science of pure geometry[17], in which there are many geometries, projective geometry, Euclidean geometry, non-Euclidean geometry, and so forth. Each of these geometries is a *model*, a pattern of ideas, and is to be judged by the interest and beauty of its particular pattern. It is a *map* or *picture*, the joint product of many hands, a partial and imperfect copy (yet exact so far as it extends) of a section of mathematical reality. But the point which is important to us now is this, that there is one thing at any rate of which pure geometries are *not* pictures, and that is the spatio-temporal reality of the physical world. It is obvious, surely, that they cannot be, since earthquakes and eclipses are not mathematical concepts.

This may sound a little paradoxical to an outsider, but it is atruism to a geometer; and I may perhaps be able to make it clearer by an illustration. Let us suppose that I am giving a lecture on some system of geometry, such as ordinary Euclidean geometry, and that I draw figures on the blackboard to stimulate the imagination of my audience, rough drawings of straight lines

[17] We must of course, for the purpose of this discussion, count as pure geometry what mathematicians call 'analytical' geometry.

orcircles or ellipses. It is plain, first, that the truth of the theorems which I prove is in no way affected by the quality of my drawings. Their function is merely to bring home my meaning to my hearers, and, if I can do that, there would be no gain in having them redrawn by the most skilful draughtsman. They are pedagogical illustrations, not part of the real subject-matter of the lecture.

Now let us go a stage further. The room in which I am lecturing is part of the physical world, and has itself a certain pattern.The study of that pattern, and of the general pattern of physical reality, is a science in itself, which we may call 'physical geometry'. Suppose now that a violent dynamo, or a massive gravitating body, is introduced into the room. Then the physicists tell us that the geometry of the room is changed, its whole physical pattern slightly but definitely distorted. Do the theorems which I have proved become false? Surely it would be nonsense to suppose that the proofs of them which I have given are affected in any way. It would be like supposing that a play of Shakespeare is changed when a reader spills his tea over a page. The play is independent of the pages on which it is printed, and 'pure geometries' are independent of lecture rooms, or of any other detail of the physical world.

This is the points of view of a pure mathematician. Applied mathematicians, mathematical physicists, naturally take a different view, since they are preoccupied with the physical world itself, which also has *it* structure or pattern. We cannot describe this pattern exactly, as we can that of a pure geometry, but we can say something significant about it. We can describe, sometimes fairly accurately, sometimes very roughly, the relations which hold between some of its constituents, and compare them with the exact relations holding between constituents of some system of pure geometry. We may be able to trace a certain resemblance between the two sets of relations, and then the pure geometry will become interesting to physicists; it will give us, to that extent, a map which 'fits the facts' of the physical world. The geometer offers to the physicist a whole set of maps from which to choose. One map, perhaps, will fit the facts better than others, and then the geometry which provides that particular map will be the geometry most important for applied mathematics. I may add that even a pure mathematician may find his appreciation of this geometry quickened, since there is no mathematician so pure that he feels no interest at all in the physical world; but, in so far as he succumbs to this temptations, he will be abandoning his purely mathematical position.

24

There is another remark which suggests itself here and which physicists may find paradoxical, though the paradox will probably seem a good deal less than it did eighteen years ago. I will express in much the same words which I used in 1922 in an address to Section A of the British Association. My audience there was composed almost entirely of physicists, and I may have spoken a little provocatively on that account; but I would still stand by the substance of what I said.

I began by saying that there is probably less difference between the positions of a mathematician and of a physicist than is generally supposed, and that the most important seems to me to be this, that the mathematician is in much more direct contact with reality. This may seem a paradox, since it is the physicist who deals with the subject-matter usually described as 'real'; but a very little reflection is enough to show that the physicist's reality, whatever it may be, has few or none of the attributes which common sense ascribes instinctively to reality. A chair may be a collection of whirling electrons, or an idea in the mind of God: each of these accounts of it may have its merits, but neither conforms at all closely to the suggestions of common sense.

I went on to say that neither physicists nor philosophers have ever given any convincing account of what 'physical reality' is, or of how the physicist passes, from the confused mass of fact or sensation with which he starts, to the construction of the objects which he calls 'real'. Thus we cannot be said to know what the subject-matter of physics is; but this need not prevent us from understanding roughly what a physicist is trying to do. It is plain that he is trying to correlate the incoherent body of crude fact confronting him with some definite and orderly scheme of abstract relations, the kind of scheme he can borrow only from mathematics.

A mathematician, on the other hand, is working with his own mathematical reality. Of this reality, as I explained in §22, I take a 'realistic' and not an 'idealistic' view. At any rate (and this was my main point) this realistic view is much more plausible of mathematical than of physical reality, because mathematical objects are so much more than what they seem. A chair or a star is not in the least like what it seems to be; the more we think of it, the fuzzier its outlines become in the haze of sensation which surrounds it; but '2' or '317' has nothing to do with sensation, and its properties stand out the more clearly the more closely we scrutinize it. It may be that modern physics fits best into some framework of idealistic philosophy—I do not believe it, but there are eminent physicists who say so. Pure mathematics, on the other hand, seems to me a rock on which all idealism founders: 317 is a prime, not because we think so, or because our minds are shaped in one way rather than another, but *because it is*, because mathematical reality is built that way.

. . . .

25

These distinctions between pure and applied mathematics are important in themselves, but they have very little bearing on our discussion of the 'usefulness' of mathematics. I spoke in §21 of the 'real' mathematics of Fermat and other great mathematicians, the mathematics which has permanent aesthetic value, as for example the best Greek mathematics has, the mathematics which is eternal because the best of it may, like the best literature, continue to cause intense emotional satisfaction to thousands of people after thousands of years. These men were all primarily pure mathematicians (though the distinction was naturally a good deal less sharp in their days than it is now); but I was not thinking only of pure mathematics. I count Maxwell and Einstein, Eddington and Dirac, among 'real' mathematicians. The great modern achievements of applied mathematics have been in relativity and quantum mechanics, and these subjects are, at present at any rate, almost as 'useless' as the theory of numbers. It is the dull and elementary parts of applied mathematics, as it is the dull and elementary parts of pure mathematics, that work for good or ill. Time may change all this. No one foresaw the applications of matrices and groups and other purely mathematical theories to modern physics, and it may be that some of the 'highbrow' applied mathematics will become 'useful' in as unexpected a way; but the evidence so far points to the conclusion that, in one subject as in the other, it is what is common place and dull that counts for practical life.

I can remember Eddington giving a happy example of the unattractiveness of 'useful' science. The British Association held a meeting in Leeds, and it was thought that the members might like to hear something of the applications of science to the 'heavy woollen' industry. But the lectures and demonstrations arranged for this purpose were rather a fiasco. It appeared that the members (whether citizens of Leeds or not) wanted to be entertained, and the 'heavy wool' is not at all an entertaining subject. So the attendance at these lectures was very disappointing; but those who lectured on the excavations at Knossos, or on relativity, or on the theory or prime numbers, were delighted bythe audiences that they drew.

26

What parts of mathematics are useful?

First, the bulk of school mathematics, arithmetic, elementary algebra, elementary Euclidean geometry, elementary differential and integral calculus. We must except a certain amount of what is taught to 'specialist', such as projective geometry. In applied mathematics, the elements of mechanics (electricity, as taught in schools, must be classified as physics).

Next, a fair proportion of university mathematics is also useful, that part of it which is really a development of school mathematics with a more finished technique, and a certain amount of the more physical subjects such as electricity and hydro mechanics. We must also remember that a reserve of knowledge is always an advantage, and that the most practical of mathematicians may be seriously handicapped if his knowledge is the bare minimum which is essential to him; and for this reason we must add a little under every heading. But our general conclusion must be that such mathematics is useful as is wanted by a superior engineer or a moderate physicist; and that is roughly the same thing as to say, such mathematics as has no particular aesthetic merit. Euclidean geometry, for example, is useful in so far as it is dull—we do not want the axiomatics of parallels, or the theory of proportion, or the construction of the regular pentagon.

One rather curious conclusion emerges, that pure mathematics is one the whole distinctly more useful than applied. A pure mathematician seems to have the advantage on the practical as well as on the aesthetic side. For what is useful above all is *technique*, and mathematical technique is taught mainly through pure mathematics.

I hope that I need not say that I am trying to decry mathematical physics, a splendid subject with tremendous problems where the finest imaginations have run riot. But is not the position of an ordinary applied mathematician in some ways a little pathetic? If he wants to be useful, he must work in a humdrum way, and he cannot give full play to his fancy even when he wishes to rise to the heights. 'Imaginary' universes are so much more beautiful than this stupidly constructed 'real' one; and most of the finest products of an applied mathematician's fancy must be rejected, as soon as they have been created, for the brutal but sufficient reason that they do not fit the facts.

The general conclusion, surely, stands out plainly enough. If useful knowledge is, as we agreed provisionally to say, knowledge which is likely, now or in the comparatively near future, to contribute to the material comfort of mankind, so that mere intellectual satisfaction is irrelevant, then the great bulk of higher mathematics is useless. Modern geometry and algebra, the theory of numbers, the theory of aggregates and functions, relativity, quantum mechanics—no one of the stands the test much better than another, and there is no real mathematician whose life can bejustified on this round. If this be the best, then Abel, Riemann, and Poincaré wasted their lives; their contribution to human comfort was negligible, and the world would have been as happy a place without them.

27

It may be objected that the concept of 'utility' has been too narrow, that I have define it in terms of 'happiness' or 'comfort' only, and have ignored the general 'social' effects of mathematics on which recent writers, with very different sympathies, have laid so much stress. Thus Whitehead (who has been a mathematician) speaks of 'the tremendous effort of mathematical knowledge on the lives of men, on their daily avocations, on the organization of society'; and Hogben (who is as unsympathetic to what I and other mathematicians call mathematics as Whitehead is sympathetic) says that 'without a knowledge of mathematics, the grammar of size and order, we cannot plan the rational society in which there will be leisure for all and poverty for none' (and much more to the same effect).

I cannot really believe that all this eloquence will do much to comfort mathematicians. The language of both writers is violently exaggerated, and both of them ignore very obvious distinctions. This is very natural in Hogben's case, since he is admittedly not a mathematician; he means by 'mathematics' the mathematics which he can understand, and which I have called 'school' mathematics. *This* mathematics has many uses, which I have admitted, which we can call 'social' if we please, and which Hogben enforces with many interesting appeals to the history of mathematical discovery. It is this which gives his book its merit, since it enables him to make plain, to many readers who never have been and never will be mathematicians, that there is more inmathematics than they thought. But he has hardly any understanding of 'real' mathematics (as any one who reads what he says about Pythagoras's theorem, or about Euclid and Einstein, can tell at one), and still less sympathy with it (as he spares no pains to show). 'Real' mathematics is to him merely an object of contemptuous pity.

It is not lack of understanding or of sympathy which is the trouble in Whitehead's cases; but he forgets, in his enthusiasm, distinctions with which he is quite familiar. The mathematics which has this 'tremendous effect' on the 'daily avocations of men' and on 'the organization of society' is not the Whitehead but the Hogben mathematics. The mathematics which can be used' for ordinary purposes by ordinary men' is negligible, and that which can be used by economists or sociologist hardly rises to 'scholarship standard'. The Whitehead mathematics may affect astronomy or physics profoundly, philosophy only appreciably—high thinking of one kind is always likely to affect high thinking of another—but it has extremely little effect on anything else. Its 'tremendous effects' have been, not on men generally, but on men like Whitehead himself.

28

There are then two mathematics. There is the real mathematics of the real mathematicians, and there is what I call the 'trivial' mathematics, for want of a better word. The trivial mathematics may be justified by arguments which would appeal to Hogben, or other writers of his school, but there is no such defence for the real mathematics, which must be justified as arts if it can be justified at all. There is nothing in the least paradoxical or unusual in this view, which is that held commonly by mathematicians.

We have still one more question to consider. We have concluded that the trivial mathematics is, on the whole, useful, and that the real mathematics, on the whole, is not; that the trivial mathematics does, and the real mathematics does not, 'do good' in a certain sense; but we have still to ask whether either sort of mathematics does *harm*. It would be paradoxical to suggest thatmathematics of any sort does much harm in time of peace, so that we are driven to the consideration of the effects of mathematics on war. It is very difficult to argue such questions at all dispassionately now, and I should have preferred to avoid them; but some sort of discussion seems inevitable. Fortunately, it need not be a long one.

There is one comforting conclusions which is easy for a real mathematician. Real mathematics has no effects on war. No one has yet discovered any warlike purpose to be served by the theory of numbers or relativity, and it seems very unlikely that anyone will do so for many years. It is true that there are branches of applied mathematics, such as ballistics and aero dynamics, which have been developed deliberately for war and demand a quite elaborate technique: it is perhaps hard to call them 'trivial', but none of them has any claim to rank as 'real'. They are indeed repulsively ugly and intolerably dull; even Littlewood could notmake ballistics respectable, and if he could not who can? So a real mathematician has his conscience clear; there is nothing to be set against any value his work may have; mathematics is, as I said at Oxford, a 'harmless and innocent' occupation.

The trivial mathematics, on the other hand, has many applications in war. The gunnery experts and aeroplane designers, for example, could not do their work without it. And the general effect of these applications is plain: mathematics facilitates (if not so obviously as physics or chemistry) modern, scientific, 'total'war.

It is not so clear as it might seem that this is to be regretted, since there are two sharply contrasted views about modern scientific war. The first and the most obvious is that the effect of science on war is merely to magnify its horror, both by increasing the sufferings of the minority who have to fight and by extending them to other classes. This is the most natural and orthodox view. But there is a very different view which seems also quite tenable, and which has been stated with great force by Haldane in *Callinicus*[18]. It can be maintained that modern warfare is *less* horrible than the warfare of pre-scientific times; that bombs are

[18] J. B. S. Haldane, *Callinicus: a Defence of Chemical Warfare* (1924).

probably more merciful than bayonets; that lachrymatory gas and mustard gas are perhaps the most humane weapons yet devised by military science; and that the orthodox view rests solely on loos-thinking sentimentalism[19]. It may also by urged (though this was not one of Haldane's theses) that the equalization of risks which science was expected to bring would be in the long range salutary; that a civilian's life is not worth more than a soldier's, nor a woman's more than a man's; that anything is better than the concentration of savagery on one particular class; and that, in short, the sooner war comes 'all out' the better.

I do not know which of these views is nearer to the truth. It is an urgent and a moving question, but I need not argue it here. It concerns only the 'trivial' mathematics, which it would be Hogben's business to defend rather than mine. The cases for his mathematics may be rather more than a little soiled; the case for mine is unaffected.

Indeed, there is more to be said, since there is one purpose at any rate which the real mathematics may serve in war. When the world is mad, a mathematician may find in mathematics an incomparable anodyne. For mathematics is, of all the arts and sciences, the most austere and the most remote, and a mathematician should be of all men the one who can most easily take refuge where, as Bertrand Russell says, 'one at least of our noblerim pulses can best escape from the dreary exile of the actual world. It is a pity that it should be necessary to make one very serious reservation—he must not be too old. Mathematics is not

---

[19] I do not wish to prejudge the question by this much misused word; it may be used quite legitimately to indicate certain type of unbalanced emotion. Many people, of course, use'sentimentalism' as a term of abuse for other people's decent feelings, and 'realism' as adisguise for their own brutality.

a contemplative but a creative subject; no one can draw much consolation from it when he has lost the power or the desire to create; and that is apt to happen to a mathematician rather soon. It is a pity, but in that case he does not matter a great deal anyhow, and it would be silly to bother about him.

29

I will end with a summary of my conclusions, but putting them in a more personal way. I said at the beginning that anyone who defends his subject will find that he is defending himself; and my justification of the life of a professional mathematician is bound to be, at bottom, a justification of my own. Thus this concluding section will be in its substance a fragment of autobiography.

I cannot remember ever having wanted to be anything but a mathematician. I suppose that it was always clear that my specific abilities lay that way, and it never occurred to me to question the verdict of my elders. I do not remember having felt, as a boy, any *passion* for mathematics, and such notions as I may have had of the career of a mathematician were far from noble. I thought of mathematics in terms of examinations and scholarships: I wanted to beat other boys, and this seemed to be the way in which I could do so most decisively.

I was about fifteen when (in a rather odd way) my ambitions took a sharper turn. There is a book by 'Alan St Aubyn'[20] called *A Fellow of Trinity*, one of a series dealing with what is supposed to be Cambridge college life. I suppose that it is a worse book than most of Marie Corelli's; but a book can hardly be entirely

[20] 'Alan St Aubyn' was Mrs Frances Marshall, wife of Matthew Marshall.

bad if it fires a clever boy's imagination. There are two heroes, a primary hero called Flowers, who is almost wholly good, and a secondary hero, a much weaker vessel, called Brown. Flowers and Brown find many dangers in university life, but the worst is a gambling saloon in Chesterton[21] run by the Misses Bellenden, two fascinating but extremely wicked young ladies. Flowers survives all these troubles, is Second Wrangler and Senior Classic, and succeeds automatically to a Fellowship (as I suppose he would have done then). Brown succumbs, ruins his parents, takes to drink, is saved from delirium tremens during a thunder storm only by the prayers of the Junior Dean, has much difficultin obtaining even an Ordinary Degree, and ultimately becomes a missionary. The friendship is not shattered by these unhappy events, and Flowers's thought stray to Brown, with affection ate pity, as he drinks port and eats walnuts for the first time in Senior Combination Room.

Now Flowers was a decent enough fellow (so far as 'Alan St Aubyn' could draw one), but even my unsophisticated mind refused to accept him as clever. If he could do these things, why not I? In particular, the final scene in Combination Room fascinated me completely, and from that time, until I obtained one, mathematics meant to me primarily a Fellowship at Trinity.

I found at once, when I came to Cambridge, that a Fellowship implied 'original work', but it was a long time before I formed any definite idea of research. I had of course found at school, as every future mathematician does, that I could often do things much better than my teachers; and even at Cambridge, I

[21] Actually, Chesterton lacks picturesque features.

found, though naturally much less frequently, that I could sometimes do things better than the College lecturers. But I was really quite ignorant, even when I took the Tripos, of the subjects on which I have spent the rest of my life; and I still thought of mathematicsas essentially a 'competitive' subject. My eyes were first opened by Professor Love, who taught me for a few terms and gave me my first serious conception of analysis. But the great debt which I owe to him—he was, after all, primarily an applied mathematician—was his advice to read Jordan's famous *Cours d'anlyse*; and I shall never forget the astonishment with which I read that remarkable work, the first inspiration for so many mathematicians of my generation, and learnt for the first time as I read it what mathematics really meant. From that time onwards, I was in my way a real mathematician, with sound mathematical ambitions and a genuine passion for mathematics.

I wrote a great deal during the next ten years, but very little of any importance; there are not more than four or five papers which I can still remember with some satisfaction. The real crisis of my career came ten or twelve years later, in 1911, when I began my long collaboration with Littlewood, and in 1913, when I discovered Ramanujan. All my best work since then has been bound up with theirs, and it is obvious that my association with them was the decisive event of my life. I still say to myself when I am depressed, and find myself forced to listen to pompous and tiresome people, 'Well, I have done one the thing *you* could never have done, and that is to have collaborated with both Littlewood and Ramanujan on something like equal terms.' It is to them that I owe an unusually late maturity: I was at my best a little past forty, when I was a professor at Oxford. Since then I have suffered from that steady deterioration which is the common fate of elderly men and particularly of elderly mathematicians. A mathematician may still be competent enough at sixty, but if it isuseless to expect him to have original ideas.

It is plain now that my life, for what it is worth, is finished, and that nothing I can do can perceptibly increase or diminish its value. It is very difficult to be dispassionate, but I count it a 'success'; I have had more reward and not less than was due to a man of my particular grade of ability. I have held a series of comfortable and 'dignified' positions. I have had very little trouble with the duller routine of universities. I hate 'teaching', and have had to do very little, such teaching as I have done been almost entirely supervision of research; I love lecturing, and have lectured a great deal to extremely able classes; and I have always had plenty of leisure for the researches which have been the one great permanent happiness of my life. I have found it easy to work with others, and have collaborated on a large scale with two exceptional mathematicians; and this has enable me to add to mathematics a good deal more than I could reasonable have expected. I have had my disappointments, like any other mathematician, but none of them has been too serious or has made me particularly unhappy. If I had been offered a life neither better nor worse when I was twenty, I would have accepted without hesitation.

It seems absurd to suppose that I could have 'done better'. I have no linguistic or artistic ability, and very little interest in experimental science. I might have been a tolerable philosopher, but not one of a very original kind. I think that I might have made a good lawyer; but journalism is the only profession, outside academic life, in which I should have felt really confident of my changes. There is no doubt that I was right to be a mathematician, if the criterion is to be what is commonly called success.

My choice was right, then, if what I wanted was a reasonable comfortable and happy life. But solicitors and stock brokers and bookmakers often lead comfortable and happy lives, and it is very difficult to see how the world is richer for their existence. Is there any sense in which I can claim that my life has been less futile than theirs? It seems to me again that there is only one possible answer: yes, perhaps, but, if so, for one reason only:

I have never done anything 'useful'. No discovery of mine has made, or is likely to make, directly or indirectly, for good or ill, the least difference to the amenity of the world. I have helped to train other mathematicians, but mathematicians of the same kind as myself, and their work has been, so far at any rate as I have helped them to it, as useless as my own. Judged by all practical standards, the value of my mathematical life is nil; and outside mathematics it is trivial anyhow. I have just one chance of escaping a verdict of complete triviality, that I may be judged tohave created something worth creating. And that I have created is undeniable: the question is about its value.

The case for my life, then, or for that of any one else who has been a mathematician in the same sense which I have been one, is this: that I have added something to knowledge, and helped others to add more; and that these somethings have a value which differs in degree only, and not in kind, from that of the creations of the great mathematicians, or of any of the other artists, great or small, who have left some kind of memorial behind them.

Note

Professor Broad and Dr. Snow have both remarked to me that, if I am to strike a fair balance between the good and evil done by science, I must not allow myself to be too obsessed by its effects on war; and that, even when I am thinking of them, I must remember that it has many very important effects besides those which are purely destructive. Thus (to take the latter point first), I must remember (*a*) that the organization of an entire population for war is only possible through scientific methods; (*b*) that science has greatly increased the power of propaganda, which is used almost exclusively for evil; and (*c*) that it has made 'neutrality' almost impossible or unmeaning, so that there are no longer 'islands of peace' from which sanity and restoration might spread out gradually after war. All this, of course, tends to reinforce the case *against* science. On the other hand, even if we press this case to the utmost, it is hardly possible to maintain seriously that the evil done by science is not altogether outweighed by the good. For example, if ten million lives were lost in every war, the net effect of science would still have been to increase the average length of life. In short, my §28 is much too 'sentimental'.

I do not dispute the justice of these criticisms, but, for the reasons which I state in my preface, I have found it impossible to meet them in my text, and content myself with this acknowledgement.

Dr. Snow had also made an interesting point about §8. Even if we grant that 'Archimedes will be remembered when Aeschylus is forgotten', is not mathematical fame a little too 'anonymous' to be wholly satisfying? We could form a fairly coherent picture of the personality of Aeschylus (still more, of course, of Shakespeare or Tolstoi) from their works alone, while Archimedes and Eudoxus would remain mere names.

Mr. J. M. Lomas put this point more picturesquely when we were passing the Nelson column in Trafalgar square. If I had a statue on a column in London, would I prefer the columns to be so high that the statue was invisible, or low enough for the features to be recognizable? I would choose the first alternative, Dr. Snow, presumably, the second.